The Anglican Way

John Baycroft was ordained to the priesthood in 1956. Since then he has served in the dioceses of Ontario and Ottawa. He is now rector of St Matthias' Church, Ottawa, and archdeacon of Ottawa West. He has written a column for the *Ottawa Journal* and lectured at Carleton University where he served as chaplain.

The Anglican Way

John Baycroft

The Anglican Book Centre
Toronto, Canada

Copyright © 1980
John Baycroft

Published by
The Anglican Book Centre
600 Jarvis Street
Toronto, Ontario
Canada M4Y 2J6

Printed in Canada
ISBN 0-919030-55-6

Contents

Introduction

This concise introductory manual of church membership is intended for enquirers, beginners, and candidates for confirmation. It is like a simple recipe on the back of a box of cake-mix. Follow the steps and you will bake a cake. Although you may not qualify immediately as a gourmet chef, you will be a baker who has made a good beginning. In this book I want to outline the basic recipe and the steps to follow in order to get a good start on church membership. You may not be a great theologian or a master of the spiritual life when you have finished reading. But there is enough here to prepare you as a real disciple and to keep you going as an active churchman, until your religious experience widens and deepens and you no longer need an introduction to church membership.

This book is not a kindergarten pamphlet dealing with things which you can outgrow and forget. All Christians in different ways need to know the two fold attraction of God and his church. And saints, bishops, church-wardens, as much as beginners, still need to live the basic Christianity of the threefold way of Bible, prayer and sacraments. I shall try to be simple and direct without oversimplifying or trivializing the faith.

Persons who become interested in church membership may have been attracted in two quite different ways. Some come because they are attracted by God. Others find that the community of the church appeals to them. From whichever direction we come to try church membership, we soon learn that the other side of church life is there and important.

The best thing the church has to offer is God. In an age when humanity has no idea where it is going, when it feels impotent in the face of overwhelming crises and helpless to defend itself against threats of mind-boggling disasters, the idea of God becomes very attractive. During the 1980s increasing numbers of people will be seeking the reality which beckons us from beyond the horizons of this world. They will want answers to fundamental questions. Is there a spiritual dimension to human life? What about the realities of love, death, and wonder? We experience these realities and are fascinated or obsessed by them, yet we cannot account for the depths of our human experience in merely human terms. In the midst of our turmoil we yearn for unity with the still centre of all that is. We may call this a quest for transcendence, or more simply, we can admit that we need God.

The church can help people who feel this need for God or who are engaged in this quest for transcendence. The church claims neither to know everything about God nor to have the answers to all human questions. But it can tell us about our Creator who loves us; it can witness to God meeting us in Jesus Christ and can teach us how to be united with God in Christ; it can show us how the Spirit of God is at work in the world and can help us to experience the same Holy Spirit at work in our own lives.

God is not a commodity dispensed by the church; rather, God takes the initiative and reaches out to us in his world. The church has experienced this divine action and love for centuries. God acts in and through his church. The church, as God's agent, can help us in our understanding and experience of his action in our lives. If, then, you want to learn about God, the church is where you can get to know him.

For some people the idea of God holds less immediate attraction than involvement with other people. They may even be embarrassed by what they regard as abstract, archaic, and unanswerable questions about God. Access to God is not a burning issue for them, but belonging to the community of the church is very appealing. The community that attracts interest may be a particular parish where there is openness to persons and to truth, love and concern for each other, acceptance of those who have failed, sensitivity to those who are hurting, and commitment to overcoming, or at least alleviating, the suffering of humanity throughout the world. The church is a community where people can become involved in social action and service. In the church we find opportunities to engage in the struggle for peace, justice, and human rights — to meet human needs and improve the human condition — without being obsessed by the problems or overwhelmed by the human dilemma.

The church is a unique community where wonder, mystery, beauty, quiet, joy, love, suffering, goodness, sin, holiness, and all other human values and experiences are taken seriously. The church is a community that stretches throughout the world. A member of the church has brothers and sisters who offer welcome and love, even though economic and cultural barriers between them seem insurmountable. The church extends through time as well as space. We can belong to a community with almost 2,000 years of history and a future that is limited only by the end of time. Even then our membership in the ''church triumphant'' is eternal. This sense of permanence gives church life a peculiar confidence and security which must not be mistaken for complacency. The church is not a cosy club, but it is great to belong to it.

Whether the newcomer is attracted by the best thing the church has to offer, which is God, or by one of the best things God has to offer, which is the community of the church, it is easy to be put off by strange language and customs. I shall try to look at some of the reasons why we talk and act as we do in the church.

The perspective of this book is Anglican and Canadian. However, Anglicans are only a part of the much wider Christian community of the one, holy, catholic, and apostolic church. We can confidently affirm the validity of the Anglican way without making pretentious or exclusive claims.

Beyond Christianity we are open to an exchange of thought and experience with people of other faiths and world-views, and we are sensitive to what we would describe as the work of the Holy Spirit among them. The Anglican Church tries to be a church in dialogue, longing for the unity of all Christian people and all mankind. Having acknowledged this, we also claim the freedom, the right, and indeed the obligation to offer to share our experience of God's action within what we call the

Anglican communion, the Anglican tradition, or the "Anglican way."

The Anglican communion is a world-wide family of autonomous, interrelated, and interdependent churches, all of which are in communion with the Archbishop of Canterbury. Anglicans speak many languages, come from many races and cultures, and are spread around the world. No small book can describe the diversity encompassed by the Anglican experience. We simply acknowledge the variety and complexity, and celebrate the richness of the Anglican communion.*

The most important thing to understand about church membership is how God offers himself to us through his church. The church draws its strength and nourishes its members from three sources: the Bible, prayer, and the sacraments. We need to understand and know exactly how to use all three of these sources.

Included are the Church of England, the Church in Wales, the Episcopal Church in Scotland, the Church of Ireland, the Church of England in Australia, Episcopal Church of Brazil (Igreja Episcopal do Brasil), the Church of the Province of Burma, the Anglican Church of Canada (L'Eglise Episcopale du Canada), the Church of the Province of Central Africa, the Church of Ceylon, the Holy Catholic Church in China (Chung Hua Sheng Kung Hui), Episcopal Church of Cuba (Iglesia Episcopal de Cuba), the Council of the Church of East Asia, the Church of the Province of the Indian Ocean, Japan Holy Catholic Church (Nippon Sei Ko Kai), Episcopal Church in Jerusalem and the Middle East, the Church of the Province of Kenya, the Church of the Province of Melanesia, the Church of

Although the Anglican Church is firmly based on the Bible, the Book of Common Prayer has become indispensable for Anglicanism. The Anglican church is a sacramental church, affirming that God works in our lives through the sacraments administered by his church. So the Anglican way is threefold. For a balanced Christianity Bible, prayer, and sacraments are essential. To ignore one of the three is like trying to sit on a three-legged stool with one leg missing. It leads to instability.

---

the Province of New Zealand, the Church of the Province of Papua New Guinea, the Church of the Province of South Africa, the Anglican Council of South America (Consejo Anglicano Sudamerica), the South Pacific Anglican Church, the Episcopal Church of the Sudan, the Church of the Province of Tanzania, the Church of the Province of Uganda, Rwanda, Burundi, and Boga-Zaire, the Episcopal Church of the United States of America, the Church of the Province of West Africa, the Church of the Province of the West Indies, and also Anglican Dioceses in Europe, Tasmania, Hong Kong and Macao, Gibraltar, Bermuda, Malaysia, Korea, Taiwan, the Phillipines, and Liberia.

The Bible

Church life draws its strength from the Bible, prayer, and the sacraments. Every beginner needs to learn to meet God in each of these three ways, because God reaches out to us in these fountains of living water. The living water is Jesus Christ, and he is God giving himself to us. A strong Christian life and a healthy Christian community will always be based on these three gifts from God that are vehicles of his self-giving.

First, we turn our attention to the Bible. An enquirer visiting an Anglican parish will quickly discover that the Bible is enormously important there. We hear it read aloud whenever we gather to worship. This reminds us that Bible study is more than just a private activity. Our attitude is important when we are trying to hear God speak to us. Listening in a congregation emphasizes that this is a community action. The Bible belongs to the community for the benefit of the community. An individualistic approach does not get us very far in Christianity, and we need the church to help us hear God's word. The Bible is explained and interpreted by preachers and teachers, and is often quoted in church discussions to give authority for a decision or to justify a course of action. Small groups of Christians often gather together for no other reason than to study the Bible together. The Bible pervades our corporate life.

Every Christian is encouraged to read the Bible regularly in private as well as to listen to it in public worship. One of the most important steps to be taken by a beginner in church membership is to become a regular reader and student of the Bible. Bible study is not difficult. But unfortunately some beginners decide to start at the beginning of the Bible and soon get discouraged. After the initial culture shock of the magnificent myths of creation, the wonderful sagas of the patriarchs, and the dramatic stories of Exodus, a reader can be confused in the wilderness of the books of Leviticus and Numbers. The very determined may persevere, find the oases, and finally win through to Revelation at the end of the New Testament. But I think most of us are better advised to read selectively.

To get started I suggest that you read one of the gospels. It does not matter which you choose, since you will eventually read all four many times. If you begin with Matthew, you will get an early treat with the Sermon on the Mount. Luke recounts some of Jesus's best parables. John is packed with profound reflections in simple language. Mark is the shortest and comes directly to the point. A good method is to read a short passage each day and think about it. Also it is helpful for a beginner to read through a whole gospel fairly quickly to get the full impact of the story.

Next, I suggest that you read one or two psalms each day. If the first one does not speak to you, then read another. We rarely need to try a third psalm before some words have caught our imagination or stimulated our thinking. The psalms also help us to talk to God. Continue your reading with the Acts of the Apostles to catch the atmosphere of the early church. Turn to Amos and learn how the moral and religious insights of a prophet in the eighth century before Christ, sound as if they were meant for the 1980s. You will now be ready for Paul's letter to the Galatians. By this stage you will be making your own selections. Perhaps you will have attended some group Bible study sessions in your parish church.

If you do not own a readable Bible, you can look over a few translations. My favourite is the Revised Standard Version, because it retains the beautiful language of the King James Version but is based upon a better text more accurately translated. It is the most reliable Bible for a serious student who does not read Hebrew and Greek. The Jerusalem Bible and the New English Bible are also excellent. Today's English Version (Good News) is very bright and readable, and the price is very reasonable. If you have more than one translation, then you can compare passages that puzzle you.

Before you buy a Bible commentary or introduction, consult your parish priest, or borrow one or two from the parish library or public library. You might try William Neil's *One Volume Bible Commentary*. There are thousands of books about the Bible, and they are not all helpful. Introductions to the Bible can sometimes intimidate us by making it sound too complicated. Mostly we need common sense and a willingness to be surprised. If we find that our understanding of what is written differs seriously from what we think the church teaches, then we need to exercise care, probe more deeply, and if necessary, get help from experts. With this in mind we can confidently read the Bible and benefit from doing so.

The word *gospel* means good news, and when you read

one of the gospels at the beginning of the New Testament, you will hear the good news about Jesus Christ. The rest of the New Testament will help you understand how the earliest Christians heard that good news, what they did about it, how it changed their beliefs, their hopes, and their lives, and how the church began. Even when he is not mentioned, the key figure on every page is Jesus Christ, who is God's living Word to us. It is in Jesus Christ that God reaches out to meet us and gives himself to us.

The Old Testament is the Hebrew Bible that Jesus knew and loved. God entered human life (became "incarnate") in a particular place, time, people, and person. We cannot understand Jesus Christ apart from the scriptures which informed his thinking as he grew up and provided the basis for his teaching as an adult. Reading the Old Testament from our Christian perspective we see the unfolding drama of God's action and revelation in human history, through the experience and insight of one particular people (the Hebrews) but for the benefit of all mankind. The culmination of this story is the New Testament.

In addition to the Old and New Testament, the Bible includes some books called the Apocrypha. Because of some dispute about their authority, they are not used to establish any church doctrine. They are good reading with lots of exciting and fascinating stories, and wise thoughts.

When you read the Bible, also use your brain. There is nothing reverent about refusing to exercise our critical faculties. If you are alert as you read, you will easily spot that some passages are poetry and some are prose. Myths, ancient legends, oral history, eyewitness accounts of actual events, ritual rules, moral laws, imaginative stories, dreams, visions, recorded teachings, editorial comment — all can be found on the pages of the Bible. God can and does speak his word to us through all these different types of material. We make it unnecessarily difficult for ourselves to hear what God is saying if we pretend that all passages in the Bible are of the same significance and if we impose upon them a narrow, rigid, and literal interpretation.

It might be better to use the plural word *scriptures* for the Bible, which comes from a Greek word meaning books. It is not one book but a collection of many books, and many of these are also compilations of older material. It all took about a thousand years to write and collect. We can treat the Bible as one book, because we see the action of God uniting all the diverse elements. Three good questions to ask in Bible study are, What could this passage have meant to the original readers and why was it written? How can the words be interpreted in our age? and above all, How does this apply to my life and situation and what am I going to do about it? You may not hear a little voice in your ear, but as the scriptures engage and influence your thoughts, God is speaking to you and you will hear his word. Christians who study in private, listen in community, or live and teach the gospel in the world, continue to experience and transmit God's word in our time.

The Bible then is the foundation of the threefold way.

Here God meets us and speaks to us in Jesus Christ. There are two other fountains of the same living water. Each provides opportunities for an encounter of the human with the divine. Neither prayer nor the sacraments exist for Christians apart from the Bible. But the Bible would be no more than a collection of ancient books if we did not receive it in the context of prayer and sacraments.

Prayer

Prayer is conversation with God. When we pray we realize our relationship with God. Although prayer uses words, it is far more than words. It includes silence, feelings, and imagination. The words are tools that help us communicate with God. Words must be used cautiously and sparingly, so that we do not spend too much time prattling to God and forget to listen to what God has to say to us. The most important part of prayer is simply being in the divine presence.

Prayer is a corporate activity of the Christian community. When the community gathers, our prayer is called public, or "common." Because the individual Christian is always a member of the church community, even when he is alone, he can continue his Christian experience in private. In private prayer we never forget the rest of the community, and we are always supported by the prayers of the whole church.

There are five ingredients in Christian prayer — adoration, penitence, petition, thanksgiving, and dedication. In *adoration* we let our minds and hearts fill with wonder and love for God who creates the universe and loves each one of us personally. In *penitence* we admit our faults, failures, sins, and weaknesses, asking for and receiving forgiveness from God. *Petition* includes both our individual concerns that we share with God and our intercessions in which we bring to God other persons and their needs. A conversation which was all asking would be a poor way to relate to God; so *thanksgiving* is also very important. When in prayer we have glimpsed God's greatness (adoration), we have been led to repentance, confession of sin, and forgiveness (penitence), we have been honest about our desires, concerns, and anxieties (petition), and we have given thanks for all our blessings (thanksgiving), then we will be lead to *dedication.* This final part of prayer is the commitment, the faith or the trust, which leads us to dedicate our lives to God and to make special resolutions about what we will do, say, and believe as a result of our prayer.

When we attend church services, we take part in public, or common, prayer. This is why the Prayer Book is officially entitled the *Book of Common Prayer.* It will help you to understand the Anglican way if you identify the elements of prayer in the services you attend. You will notice a skilful blending of all the essential ingredients. Adoration and penitence, petition and intercession, thanksgiving and dedication all join in a balanced structure.

In your private prayers you can arrange the ingredients and mix them as you wish. Some people get a lot of help from formal printed prayers taken either from the Prayer Book or from the many books of private prayer and devotion. It is a good idea to make your own collection of prayers in a note book. Others prefer to rely on memorized prayers or on spontaneous prayer, using their own wording when words are needed. Perhaps the best way is to use all these sources.

The Anglican way encourages regular private prayer for all but leaves us free to work out our own pattern and timing for prayer. Each morning we should say at least a brief good morning to God and remember that he will be with us through the day. Each evening we should at least briefly commit ourselves into God's care. Either in the morning or the evening, or when convenient, we should plan for a longer period of prayer. This will become our daily quiet time and can often be combined with Bible reading.

Your daily extended and systematic prayer might be organized as follows. Pick a time and place where you will be undisturbed for fifteen minutes. (Five minutes may be enough for you at first.) It does not matter whether you sit, kneel, stand, or walk, so long as you are comfortable and able to concentrate. You can experiment with different postures. Close your eyes and imagine a scene which fills you with wonder. A clear starlit night, the sea, the mountains, the forest, sunlight reflecting on the surface of a lake — such pictures can focus the mind and fill the soul with a sense of wonder, beauty, and the majesty of God. Imagining a scene from the gospels or looking at a crucifix, statue, or religious painting can also help.

I knew a priest who built a very beautiful chapel in his imagination. He knew every detail of its appearance and exactly how it felt to be in it. When he wanted to pray he simply closed his eyes and thought of himself opening the chapel door, walking in, and kneeling down. By the time he was kneeling, his mind was also settling down and he was already praying. Another effective way to achieve quietness inside ourselves, after we have made an opportunity for quiet on the outside, is to remember a few bars of beautiful music, perhaps, but not necessarily, church music. I like to imagine myself walking on the shore where sea and land meet. In one way or another, allow yourself to become quiet.

In the quiet, think of God's majesty and love. One day you might concentrate on the beauty of creation. On another occasion you might think of the sacrificial love that is demonstrated in the suffering of Jesus. At other times you might reflect on the mystery of the divine Spirit's presence in the depth of our being. Do not strain over this adoration. It is sufficient to take a few moments to allow your consciousness to flow around the exciting yet strangely tranquil mystery of God. Even the very simple thought that the Creator of all has a personal interest in you, is sufficient to stir wonder which is the beginning of adoration.

After trying to focus your mind upon God and goodness, the next stage of prayer is allowing your attention to turn to yourself. When we have been aware of God's glory and perfection, when we have looked at the perfect human example of Jesus, and when we have thought about the opportunity given us by the Holy Spirit within us, we are bound to feel that we have fallen far short of God's standard and are neither what we could be nor what we should be. Knowing that we are in conversation with God, from whom there are no secrets, helps us to be honest about ourselves and with ourselves. Being honest does not mean wallowing in guilt. You should not learn to enjoy your status as a sinner. Dealing with our sins in prayer is like putting out the garbage; it is necessary but incidental to the main activity, which is communion with God. A form of self examination might help, providing you do not become obsessed with a check list approach to sin spotting.

Try the following exercise. Read 1 Corinthians 13 in the New Testament. Then re-read the description of charity, or love, from verse four to the beginning of verse eight. Next read the passage again, substituting the word *Jesus* for the word *love.* Finally re-read it with the words *Do I?* and *Am I?* substituted for *love.* There are many other techniques of self-examination. The whole point of the exercise is to face and confess the truth about ourselves, so that we can be freed from the failures, the mistakes, and the evil of our past by God's love and forgiveness. Then with our minds turned in the right direction, we can try again to live a new and Christ-like life with God's help. With sin out of the way the major obstacle to communication with God is removed.

Next you should ask God for whatever you believe is appropriate. This includes petitions for ourselves and intercessions for others. Some people write out a prayer list to spread the intercessions over a week. Feel free to tell God your particular need or concern. If it is important to you, then it belongs in your conversation with God. He is never too busy. God is not a harassed bank teller prevented from friendly conversation by a long line of impatient customers behind you. He is infinite and all-loving. Of course you may hesitate to ask God about something because you know in your heart it is wrong.

You should still talk to God about it. If you do not already know, you will soon discover that prayer is not magic. There is no formula which enables us to manipulate God's power. Yet countless Christians through the ages testify that God has heard and answered their prayers, not always as they expected or wished, but always as was best.

Prayer is far more than a mental-health exercise. Nevertheless a good deal of it is great therapy. When we count all our blessings and say thank you to God, it is amazing how much better we feel. It is good to be specific in prayer. To say, "Thank you, God, for everything," is better than to say nothing, but not much better. So try to think of some particular cause for thankfulness when you pray, and occasionally try to list all your reasons for thanksgiving.

Finally our prayer should lead us to faith and trust, and commitment of our lives to God our Father. When we pray, we should try each day to make at least one definite resolution which springs from our experience of being with God in prayer. This is the ingredient called dedication.

The model suggested above is just one design for daily prayer. If it seems too complicated, perhaps you should try saying the Lord's Prayer slowly and frequently, thinking about your heavenly Father who loves you and knows all the secrets of your heart. He wants you to know him better and to be at ease in conversation with him. You could also try quietly repeating a short Bible passage that makes a simple statement of faith (for example, "I am with you always''). Do not worry about what you do not understand. No one understands everything about God. Whatever method you use, go slowly to let God influence your thoughts; don't race through a prescribed form.

I do not think it is bad if your time of private prayer drifts off into sanctified daydreaming. If, like myself, you find that many books and people who talk about prayer seem to speak from an elevation which you neither expect nor desire to attain, you might be encouraged by recalling that prayer is conversation with God. Since he is omnipotent, let him do most of the work. It was his idea. Simply make yourself available regularly and believe that something is happening. God does act in our lives, but we often go for long stretches without being able to detect anything much. Also rely on common prayer, the prayer of the church. Join the stream of the community's prayer, and let it carry you along with it. You are not expected to practise Christianity alone.

The Sacraments

In the Anglican way we draw freely from all three wells of living water. We now discuss the third fountain, the sacraments. As in prayer and the Bible, so also in the sacraments, God reaches out and offers himself to us through Jesus Christ by the activity of his Holy Spirit.

A sacrament is "an outward and visible sign of an inward and spiritual grace, given to us by Christ himself, as a means whereby we receive this grace, and a pledge to assure us thereof" (Canadian Prayer Book, page 550). In the traditional teaching and practice of the church there are seven sacraments. Two of the seven tower in importance over the other five. All seven are means of God's grace (*grace* means free gift), and through all of them God reaches out to us and enters our lives.

All Christians are agreed on the necessity of the two great sacraments of holy baptism and the Holy Eucharist. Catholic Christianity also offers the five sacraments of confirmation, penance (confession and absolution), holy matrimony, holy unction, and holy orders.

Baptism

Baptism is the sacramental beginning of the Christian life. The outward part of baptism is the water in which a person is baptized "in the name of the Father, and of the Son, and of the Holy Spirit." What cannot be seen is "the inward and spiritual grace," or what God is giving to, or doing for, the recipient. We can describe the inward part of baptism as a new birth (regeneration), for it is the beginning of a new life as a child of God in the family of the church. A more profound description of baptism is to say that it is a death and resurrection. The candidate is united with Christ and enters into the experience of his dying and rising again. What happened to Christ becomes part of the Christian's own life and memory. Christ's story is now the believer's story, and the Christian is part of Christ. When a baptism is done, as it was originally, by total immersion, it is easy to see how it represents a death and then a new life. The water of baptism also symbolizes the washing away of all sins. All of these ways of describing baptism point to God's gift to us of a new life. We are set free from the past and united with Jesus Christ to live and love in his Spirit.

To become a Christian and a member of the Christian community one must be baptized. Baptism is the sacramental incorporation of the believer into the body of Christ (see page 53) and the beginning of a new life in Christ.

Although the focus in baptism is on what God does for us, this is not magic. We do not control God, but his free gift calls for our response. Baptism makes requirements of us, namely repentance and faith. (We have already said a little about repentance when we were discussing prayer, and we shall have more to say later. Faith, or belief and trust in the one, holy, and undivided Trinity, the Father, the Son, and the Holy Spirit, will also be discussed later in this book.) The quickest way to begin to understand baptism is to think of it happening to adults who, of course, are capable of repentance and faith. Infants are baptized in the Anglican Church on the clear understanding that they will be brought up to follow Jesus Christ and to reject evil, in the family and faith of the Christian church, learning the meaning of what happened in baptism. An extremely individualistic approach to religion would have difficulty in making sense of baptizing tiny babies. But the Anglican way makes sense because of the tremendous power and importance of the community of persons through which God nurtures the baptized infant. Baptism is the sacramental beginning of the Christian life in the Christian community for both children and adults.

If you have not been baptized you should approach a parish priest and ask for his help in preparing for baptism, so that you can start as soon as possible on the pilgrimage of the Christian life.

Holy Eucharist

The Holy Eucharist is the sacramental centre of the Christian life. Although baptism is important, it is only the beginning. Christian growth continues throughout our lives. Our growth is nurtured by, and our Christian lives are centred on, the Holy Eucharist. In Anglicanism the Holy Eucharist, like Christ, has many names. Eucharist (which means thanksgiving), Holy Communion, the Lord's Supper, Mass, and the Blessed Sacrament are the most common names for the sacred act that our Lord himself instituted the night before he died on the cross. You can learn a lot about this sacrament by reading the order for the Holy Eucharist and the catechism in the Prayer Book. You will learn even more by regular attendance at the Eucharist.

The outward part of the Holy Eucharist is bread and wine. The inward part is the Body and Blood of Christ. Clearly we are talking about how we share Christ's life as members of his body.

The Eucharist always includes a service of the *word*, when we listen to what God has to say to us through the Bible. It also includes public *prayer,* where you will find all the ingredients we have already mentioned. Then, distinguishing it from all other services and sacraments, there are four great acts involving the bread and wine. First of all there is the *offertory*, when the bread and wine are offered to God. They represent our lives, our concerns, and the whole created order, and they are offered in union with the offering of Jesus Christ on the cross. The next great act is *consecration,* the blessing, when God takes what we offer through Jesus Christ and makes it holy. The third act is the *breaking* of bread. This was originally functional (so that one loaf could be shared), but it is also symbolic, linking Jesus' breaking bread at the last supper, his voluntary offering of his body on the cross, and our participation with him in the eucharistic sacrifice. The fourth great act is *communion,* when God shares his life with us through the bread and wine, which have been united with Christ's life to become for us his Body and Blood, his giving of himself to us and for us.

There are two important dimensions to this eucharistic

action. First, we remember, re-enact, and participate in the great acts of redemption and salvation history. In the Holy Eucharist we recall and share in Christ's death and resurrection. Secondly, we recognize that the bread and wine become for us the Body and Blood of Christ because of the action of the Holy Spirit. In the Holy Eucharist we pray to the Father through Jesus Christ, and this is effective because his Holy Spirit is at work in the church, in the sacrament, and in us.

The church exists to glorify God and to feed his people. The Eucharist is our central act of worship. It is also our primary way of being fed. In the church's family meal we know that, faithful to his promise, Christ shares his life with us by feeding us with the bread and wine which have become his Body and Blood through the action of the Holy Spirit. This is why our liturgy talks about receiving the spiritual food of the most precious Body and Blood. The church could not live without the Eucharist. The Eucharist is always presided over by a bishop, who is a successor of the apostles with whom Christ instituted this sacrament, or by a priest ordained by a bishop to assist him in his apostolic ministry.

The two basic and essential sacraments of baptism and Eucharist show how down to earth Christianity is. We boldly affirm that God acts in our lives at identifiable times in specific ways. God makes us Christians and saves us in baptism. God unites us with himself and his church, and feeds us in Holy Communion. This super-confidence that characterizes the Christian faith, is rooted in our belief that God acts in human history, that he takes humanity into his divinity in the incarnation, and that his Spirit lives in the church and in the individual Christian. Because we live in a material world, God reaches out to us in material ways in the concrete sacraments.

Confirmation

Confirmation is the apostolic rite of the laying on of hands on those who are baptized. In the case of those who are baptized as infants, Anglicans usually delay the laying on of hands until a person is old enough to understand the difference between right and wrong, to acknowledge the value of faith, and to renew willingly and consciously the vows of baptism and receive the gifts of the Spirit to live an adult Christian life. Strictly speaking there is no theological reason why an infant should not be confirmed at the time of baptism. But most Anglicans prefer to delay confirmation to allow time for the growth of a conscious response of personal faith. Anglicans insist on the presence of a bishop to officiate in confirmation, and on the action of the laying on of hands. Confirmation could be performed by a priest authorized by the bishop and using oil blessed by him. It could be, but so far it is not. We generally prefer our familiar and traditional way. The catechism and order for confirmation in the Prayer Book explain more about this sacrament.*

In many dioceses and parishes church members do not receive Holy Communion until after they have been confirmed. But

If you have not been confirmed by a bishop, you should approach your parish priest. Preparation for confirmation allows us to reach the point where we can commit our lives to Christ in the family of the church and open ourselves to the gifts of the Holy Spirit. After our public witness and commitment we believe that we are indeed strengthened by the Holy Spirit when the bishop lays his hands on our heads with prayer.

Penance

The sacrament of penance, or confession and absolution, is available in the Anglican communion but is not as widely used as it ought to be. Sacramental confession takes place when an individual makes a private confession of his sins in the presence of a priest. When it is appropriate, the priest may give advice; but more important, he is able to pronounce absolution in such a way that the penitent can feel completely confident and

---

because baptism is the complete and final initiation of the Christian into the church (the eucharistic community), other parts of our church have decided to admit persons, including young children, to communion before confirmation. This is done with the approval of the bishop, provided that persons coming to communion are baptized, can make a simple affirmation of faith, and have been instructed in the meaning and practice of receiving the Holy Communion. When persons who are already communicants come to confirmation, it is seen very clearly as an act of commitment and a sacrament of the Spirit empowering the believer for service in the church and the world.

assured of God's forgiveness. This sacrament is very helpful when some particular sin or a persistent sense of unworthiness and guilt is getting in the way of a person's relationship with God. The Anglican rule about sacramental confession is that everybody *may*, nobody *must*, and some people *should* make their confession with a priest in this way. When we tell another human being about our sins, secrets, and innermost thoughts, we are encouraged to deal with them honestly. The experience of our continuing acceptance by the representative of God and the church, and the absolution pronounced in God's name, bring a feeling of liberation and an awareness of new life. We are given a fresh start.

Holy Matrimony

The sacrament of holy matrimony is well known. The church believes that marriage is part of God's purpose for mankind and that in a lifelong community of self-giving love, human sexuality reflects the mystery of divine love. The ideal environment for the nurture of children is a family where the husband and wife give themselves to each other in love.

The church tries to provide careful pastoral preparation for marriage. In human terms a church wedding affirms the permanence and fullness of the commitment, and the completeness of the mutual giving and sharing. In sacramental terms the marriage, which of course continues long after the wedding ceremony, is a sign of the divine self-giving love and is sustained by that love. The wedding is supported by the love and prayers of the Christian community, which in turn benefits from the renewing experience of being reminded of the vows, standards, and blessings of Christian marriage. If possible, a wedding should take place in the context of the Eucharist.

Holy Unction

The sacrament of holy unction is the anointing with oil and prayer for those who are sick. It is not widely used but has seen a revival in recent years. The ministry to the sick and prayers for healing are very important in the Anglican way. It is very common to take Holy Communion to people who are ill and unable to attend the public worship of the church. For many this has seemed sufficient sacramental help without holy unction. Unction is an ancient sacrament with a biblical basis (James 5:14), and is provided for in the Canadian Prayer Book (page 585).

Holy Orders

The sacrament of holy orders is not received by every Christian, but it is important to all church members. Because the church is a community of persons and because God is personal, God works through persons to help other persons and to serve the community. As Christ chose apostles, so the church has continued to set apart successors to the apostles. The line of bishops, who are consecrated (ordained) by other bishops, stretches back in time to the apostles and provides our historical link with the church founded by Christ. They safeguard both our continuity and faithfulness to the gospel. Bishops, through other bishops, also form our link with the world-wide church. The bishops ordained other sacred ministers to assist them in the apostolic ministry. The two other orders in the ordained sacred ministry of the church are priests and deacons.

A bishop is the chief pastor in a diocese and is responsible for the ministry of the word and sacraments, and the good discipline and sound teaching of the church. He can administer all seven sacraments. A priest may administer baptism, the Holy Eucharist, penance, matrimony, and unction, but may not ordain or confirm. The deacon's ministry is focussed on the service of those in special need and the ministry of the word. The sacramental role of the deacon is usually to assist a bishop or priest. In the absence of a priest or bishop, the deacon may baptize and, in very special circumstances, perform weddings.

All three holy orders of bishops, priests, and deacons are important in catholic churches, including the Anglican communion. The Anglican Church of Canada is one of the churches in the Anglican communion where women can be ordained. The aim of the ordained ministry is to serve God and his people as Christ the servant serves. The clergy are therefore often seen as Christ's representatives. Their primary functions are to glorify God, to lead people in his worship, and to build up and nurture the church.

We have now surveyed the Anglican threefold way. There is so much offered to us in these three fountains of living water that we may feel overwhelmed. But we should remember that they provide for our needs during a whole life-time and also for the needs of all men throughout the world and throughout history. Obviously there is more offered than any one person can absorb. But we can begin to accept all that God has to offer if we continually open ourselves to God, by learning all three ways of Bible, prayer, and sacrament.

God

You will have noticed that God is repeatedly described as Father, Son, and Holy Spirit. Christians believe in the Holy Trinity (meaning tri-unity), three in one and one in three, one holy and undivided Trinity, three persons and one God. To be honest we have to admit that many people today claim to find this language hopelessly confusing and completely mystifying.

It helps when we discover the precise meaning of the words, especially those that have changed their meaning in modern English. For example, if we mistakenly suppose that *person* means "individual," then we have a mathematical puzzle and not a divine disclosure. You may want to pursue the historical meanings of trinitarian language in a book of fundamental theology. But perhaps it is easier to understand the way the church talks about God when we recognize that human language can never define God. You cannot put a gallon of beer in a pint pot, and that which is infinitely greater cannot be contained in that which is lesser. Some of our difficulties arise not because our knowledge and intelligence are too limited for us to understand what someone much wiser and more learned is saying, but simply because words cannot do justice to the reality which is God. On the other hand, having admitted the impossibility of defining God in words, we should acknowledge the church's marvellous achievement in expressing with remarkable simplicity the doctrine of the Trinity which is the greatest of all mysteries.

The first part of belief in the Holy Trinity is belief and trust in God the Father who made the world. Notice how we combine a belief that God is the source and creator of all that is, with the belief that God is personal and relates to us as our Father. When we think of God as creator, we do not reduce him to a vast impersonal creative principle. Since his creation includes persons, the creator must be at least personal, or he would be less than what he created. We believe that he has revealed to us something about himself as person and that this is best described as a loving parent, or as Jesus taught us, "our Father."

When we analyse the religious experience of Christians through the centuries, and of their Old Testament predecessors, we get a very clear idea of the personal God. First, God makes moral demands of his children. Because the demand is from God, it is experienced as absolute demand. When we believe that a course of action is God's will, we are faced with an imperative that requires our absolute obedience. We attach the concept of father to this absolute demand. Totally different from the tyranny of an arbitrary despot, the parental love which makes demands upon children is necessary for a child's healthy growth and development. God's moral demand is part of his creativity. When we ignore his demand we contribute to the destructive forces at work in our lives. Obedience to the moral imperative is creative.

Secondly, in the Bible and Christian tradition, God is experienced as helper, friend, support, protector, the source of all strength and nourishment. In other words God's love is not only absolute demand but also ultimate succour. God loves his children simply because they are his children, and nothing can destroy that love. While his absolute demand calls us to our perfection, his ultimate succour rescues us when we fail, sets us free to begin again, and empowers us as we grow in goodness.*

All that is comes from God; all that is goes to God; all that is is sustained by God. He is Being. We have admitted that human and personal language cannot define God, who transcends all our experience. But using our limited experience, we can claim that Being itself has chosen to reveal itself to us in a loving and personal way. Therefore we walk in this world with cosmic confidence. We do not understand all about this world, but we do trust that, whatever happens, we are in the hands of our loving Father.

The second part of our trinitarian faith is belief and trust in God's Son, Jesus Christ who redeems (liberates) mankind. (If you are not sure why humanity needs liberation or redemption, I shall try to explain when we come to chapter 7 on salvation.)

Our language about God is not intended to attribute to him either maleness or sexuality. Clearly our experience of absolute demand is related to the father symbol and what some psychologists call paternal love. Ultimate succour relates to the mother and maternal love. Even in human terms this distinction is artificial, because males and females need to experience and express both kinds of love. With reference to God, love is both maternal and paternal, transcending the sexual distinction. Neither God nor good theology is male chauvinist.

The first disciples met Jesus in Palestine almost 2,000 years ago. When they met him, it never occurred to them that he might be anything other than a human being. That is because he was human. Until their dying day none of the disciples or apostles ever denied that Jesus was a man. However, they also came to the belief, which they proclaimed around the world, that Jesus Christ was divine. This belief in the divinity of Christ began during his earthly ministry. The first disciples lived in a religious culture. They knew how to pray and trusted that God loved them. They believed that he had revealed his will to them in the scriptures. They had a vital faith in God. Then they met Jesus. As he taught, they felt that they were hearing God's will revealed more clearly and directly than ever before. When they were with Jesus, they were aware of the closeness and presence of God and his love, which exceeded anything they had known in private prayer, synagogue, or temple. For them God was the liberator, the redeemer, who brought his people out of bondage in Egypt. When they were with Jesus they began to experience a freedom to love, a liberation from fear, and a confidence that they were empowered to overcome evil.

The growing conviction that God was meeting them in Jesus must have suffered a severe blow when he was crucified and they saw him dead and buried. But their doubts disappeared when they met him again, risen from the dead. The living Christ convinced the disciples that God had entered human life in Jesus. It was some years before the doctrines of the Trinity and the two natures of

Christ were expressed as clearly as we have them. But the earliest disciples were convinced of both the humanity and the divinity of Christ by their own experience.

In Christ's death and resurrection we see that nothing can deter or defeat God's love and that he is victorious over fear, evil, and death. By uniting us with himself in Jesus Christ, God enables us to share his victory; we are set free, liberated, or redeemed. United with Christ we are not only free but also new men. The risen life of Christ, which we share, is divine as well as human and is therefore eternal. Belief and trust in Jesus Christ means trusting his way of self-giving love and following him in our daily lives. We become disciples. Being a disciple is far more important than being an Anglican. While it is not the only way, the Anglican way is a good way of Christian discipleship.

Some people find it hard to believe that God would become incarnate in a particular human being in history. If we can believe that this world is created by a personal God, and that God loves his creation and creatures, then we can believe that God's love will reach out to us in a way that we can receive. That is what God does in Jesus Christ. In Christ, God meets us in the perfect union of himself with a human person. Jesus Christ is perfect God and perfect man.

The third part of belief in the triune God is belief and trust in the Holy Spirit, who sanctifies (makes holy) the people of God. If we only talk about God as Father and Son, we fail to describe an enormously important and intimate part of our experience of God. If we describe the

Father as over us, and Jesus Christ as God with us, then the Spirit is God in us. God meets us and we experience his presence and activity in the very depths of our being. The inspiration of the Holy Spirit, like breath for natural life, is a necessity for spiritual life. Inspiration from God is also indwelling by God. God the Holy Spirit lives in the Christian and gives him or her the strength, wisdom, courage, hope, and love to live a Christ-like life.

There is no "magic" in Christianity. Human response and acceptance of God's offer is necessary. We need to be willingly open to the Holy Spirit, to believe that God truly lives within us, and to trust his Spirit within us. Many of us are too humble to trust the Spirit. We are willing to believe that God's Spirit inspired and empowered Saint Peter or Saint Paul, but we do not presume to put ourselves in that class. Belief in the Holy Trinity destroys this misleading modesty. We diminish God if we refuse to believe that he is able and willing to work in any human life.

When we believe and trust in God's Spirit at work in us, we develop a divine self-confidence. We know that whatever situation we face, God is with us to give us the strength to do his will, to help us when we fail, and to hold us in his love. We also develop reverence toward our fellow human beings who, like us, are temples of the Holy Spirit. Not everything we hear from one of the Holy Spirit's temples (another Christian) is going to be the word of God. But we do well to listen to each other, because the Spirit can and does speak to us through the lips of fellow Christians. Respect for the Spirit at work in others helps prevent us from trying to dominate or manipulate persons' lives.

The activity of God as Spirit must not be understood in a fragmented and individualistic way. The Spirit is at work in a community of persons. Each person in the Spirit-filled community receives the Spirit's gifts for the benefit of the whole community. So we speak of the fellowship of the Holy Spirit. The Holy Spirit is always experienced by human beings as a gift. If you think about it, you will be able to identify some of the Spirit's gifts in your life. In doing this be prepared for surprises. One of the reasons why we sometimes use the symbol of wind for the Spirit, is to acknowledge the element of surprise in God's activity within us which, from our point of view, is unpredictable and often not at all what we expect.

My impresion is that many church members are more at ease thinking about the first and second persons of the Holy Trinity than about the third. If you feel like this, try using the hymn "Come Holy Ghost, our souls inspire" slowly as a prayer, every day for a month. (You will find it on page 653 in the Prayer Book.) If you have not been confirmed, then you should prepare for the sacrament of confirmation and receive the gifts of the Holy Spirit through the prayers of the church and the laying on of hands by the bishop. If you are already confirmed, you may find it helpful in your daily prayers to use the five line confirmation prayer "Defend, O Lord . . ." (page 560 in the Prayer Book). As with the rest of the doctrine of the Trinity, belief in the Holy Spirit only makes good sense when we have experienced the reality we talk about.

We talk about the Trinity because that is how we believe God reveals himself to us. Since God would not deceive us, we are confident that the divine threefold nature that we describe, expresses the reality of God as he is, although we must repeat that the language we use can never do justice to God. Our faith can be expressed in few words. The Anglican Church believes and teaches the faith expressed concisely in the historic creeds. You should memorize and think about the Apostles' Creed. You will also learn the Nicene Creed through repeated use of it in the Holy Eucharist. In thinking about the creeds you will reflect on the church's central doctrines of creation, incarnation, atonement, resurrection, the coming of the Holy Spirit, the church, and the last things.

We are made sufficiently like our divine creator to be able to enter into a loving relationship with him. In order to love, persons must be free. Therefore we are created free and can choose to love God and each other or to reject love. The misuse of freedom leads to its loss, and the failure to love has destructive results. But God's love does not fail. In order to bridge the gap between us, which has widened through our continuing rejection of love, God enters human life in Christ (incarnation). In Christ God makes us at one with himself in love (at-one-ment, atonement). Such love is costly and requires total self-giving, which we see in the crucifixion. There total self-giving love is poured out freely; death is accepted but overcome. This true love is true life. Resurrection is not only for Christ but for all who receive and share his life and love. The Holy Spirit comes into our lives to make the divine life and love present within us. The church is the sphere where the new life, for which we are created, can be experienced in a community of persons who are reconciled to God and set free to love. Our experience of this new life of love, in harmony with our fellows and with God, is only fragmentary in this world. So we look forward with hope to the unbroken experience of complete harmony with God, when the experiment of creation will be successful.

Within the context of our traditional faith we grasp and are grasped by the fundamental obsessive realities which fascinate and trouble men and women of all times and places. The great questions and experiences such as love, death, and wonder should not be ignored, diminished, falsified, or avoided, as is too often the case in materialism and secularism. In the Anglican Church you will learn about the love of God and man; you will be set free to love and be helped to love; you will also be loved. Even a reality we often fear, such as death, is not hidden. A Christian in the community of life and love can handle death and his feelings about death. We are helped to die and find life. We can experience the bitterness of bereavement and loneliness, and discover hope and joy in fellowship with God and each other.

Church life encourages wonder. We should not be ashamed of being religious. Religion has nothing to do with superstition, fanaticism, credulity, or prejudice. It is a perfectly reasonable way to respond to the whole of life, including the spiritual dimension. We are willing to be open to all truth, including God's revelation of himself to us. In worship we see life as a whole from the perspective of eternity. In principle nothing is omitted and everything is included. Worship is the only human activity which allows us to experience this sense of wholeness. We believe we need to talk about God if we are to give an account of the whole of reality. We need to worship if we are to enter into a relationship with all that is, the totality of being.

The Church

People matter. The church is a community of people that care about people. Pastoral care springs from a concern for the well-being of the whole person and the community. The Anglican Church places a heavy emphasis on the pastoral dimension of church life. Because God loves persons, his church must express that love. If the church fails to be an agent of the divine love, no words can make up for that failure. The pastoral care of the church for all people is the responsibility of every church member. Every member is also cared for by the church. In a sense there is a shepherd and a sheep in each of us.

The church's care for persons is particularly helpful at times of need, like sickness, bereavement, death, or when we fail and hurt ourselves or each other. It is also important at joyful peak experiences, like births or marriages, when there is a heightened sensitivity to the spiritual dimension of human life. But it also embraces the whole of our lives, including the times of unremarkable growth and slow change.

The sacraments of the church are all administered within the context of caring for persons. One of the reasons why we have conspicuous buildings scattered all over the country is to make the pastoral care of the church freely available to all people. Anglicans respect the religious and denominational choices of others. But in order to express the truth that God's love knows no limits and is for all, every person on earth is potentially under the pastoral responsibility of a bishop. Obviously in Canada it is easier to find out who that bishop is, and which your local parish is, than it would be in some other countries. Your parish priest is available to you whether or not you are an Anglican. He is responsible for every person inside his parish boundaries.

The distinctive gifts which the church has to offer are the Bible, prayer, and the sacraments. Parishes also express God's love with all kinds of acts of human kindness, friendship, and service. Jesus Christ lived on earth as a servant of his fellow men. The church continues his presence in the world as a serving community. While we serve individuals one by one, we must also be concerned about the society in which we live. Unless society is just, individuals will suffer. "Ambulance work" with the victims of injustice is not sufficient. So the church is also engaged in the struggle for social justice. We seek to build a loving community where God will rule as King in the hearts and lives of persons. Since society has so many problems, the church is active on many fronts. Racism, native rights, bio-ethics, poverty, third world development are a random few of the many areas in which you can become involved through the church. However, we are a community of persons who support each other and share the work. You, as an individual, do not have to be active on all fronts at once.

The church helps us to make moral choices. Christians promise to reject evil and to do the will of God. We strive for goodness. The question, What ought I to do? is therefore very important to us. Anybody who has asked this question knows it is sometimes extraordinarily difficult to answer. We are moral agents, and we cannot divest ourselves of responsibility for our decisions. The church can help but cannot become a moral dictator and simply tell us what to do. A member will look to the church for guidance, inspiration, and example but must finally obey his conscience. God's moral demand is absolute, and once we are convinced in our conscience that God's will is clear, then we must obey. What, however, are we to do when God's will is not clear to us?

The Bible is a rich source of moral teaching. You should learn the Ten Commandments (Exodus 20) and become thoroughly familiar with the Sermon on the Mount (Matthew 5–7). It is very important for a Christian to remember that he makes his moral decisions as a part of Christ's body. So the moral question becomes, What do I think Jesus Christ would do, think, say, if he were in this situation? or What would Jesus avoid doing, saying, thinking, when faced with these alternatives?

Some people are helped by applying a love ethic. They try to discover what is the most loving course of action and follow that. This is an excellent approach which frees us from a legalistic attitude to living. Unfortunately the question of what is the most loving action is frequently as difficult as what is the right action. Another approach is to do our morality from the inside out. Become a good, loving, honest, fair, thoughtful character and your behaviour will express your character. It will be natural to do the right. Christianity relies heavily on this approach, but there are still situations where we are not sure we have the right answer.

Remember what we said earlier about penitence in prayer and in the sacrament of penance. God provides us with the possibility of new beginnings even after we have made wrong choices. If we ask God to guide us, if we are trying to love as he loves, if we trust his power and presence in our lives, then we shall probably do the right thing. Moral courage is a virtue which includes the willingness to risk being wrong. If we are mistaken in a decision but are willing to admit the error, then we shall be brought back to the right way. God is not giving us a proficiency test in an obstacle course. He is loving us. Our moral choices are ways we grow in receiving, returning, and sharing his love.

The church is described in the Nicene Creed as one, holy, catholic, and apostolic (the Prayer Book, page 72). Since the church is God's church and the body of Christ, there can obviously be only *one* church as we say in the Creed. The Anglican communion, therefore, can only be a small part of the one church. We are committed to seeking visible unity on earth with other Christians.

The church is *holy* because it belongs to God. We try to express this holiness in our institutions and organization, to practise it in our programs and activities, and to demonstrate it in our individual Christian lives. We are not always conspicuously successful. But because we belong to God and holiness is a gift from him, we are not discouraged. In a sense we are already holy, and when God has completed his work in us, that holiness will show.

Catholic means universal, all-inclusive, embracing all.

We believe that the church should be consistent with the divine love which it expresses, and which is catholic, reaching out to all and excluding none. The catholic church, like God's love, is open to men, women, and children of all races, classes, and cultures. *Catholic* should not be used as a label to distinguish one group of Christians from another, although we might wish to use it for Christians who are in communion with the Catholic Church and who hold the catholic faith.

To be *apostolic* means to be sent by God with a mission. Historically the church was founded by Jesus Christ, and he entrusted to the apostles the leadership and nurture of the church in the mission that he began. Bishops, who are believed by Anglicans to be the historic successors of the apostles, ensure the continuity and continuation of the church's faith, life, and work. Not only the episcopate (the bishops) but also the whole church is apostolic, since the whole church is sent by God. Every Christian ought to be in mission, taking God's love into God's world.

In the Bible Paul powerfully describes the church as the body of Christ. We take this very seriously. A member of a body obeys the head and works in harmony with the other members, depending upon, serving, and respecting them. Christ unites the human and divine in one body. So in his body, the church, we have the meeting of the human and the divine. The Prayer Book teaches that the church has a twofold role, to glorify God and to edify his people. The church's primary purpose is worship, and we are a worshipping community. In worship we experience the encounter of God and man. This is natural in a community which is the body of Christ.

In this chapter we have moved rather quickly from the humanitarian to the theological viewpoint, and it should be clear that the church does not regard herself as a merely human institution. We are a divinely ordained, Spirit-filled community of persons. Sometimes Anglicans are accused of placing the church before its Lord. But because the church is the body of Christ, there is no real opposition. The Anglican way, however, does place great emphasis on the community of the church.

Salvation

Although no honest and realistic approach to human life can ignore sin and evil, many people do not appear to take sin very seriously. Unless we understand what the church teaches about sin and salvation, we shall probably ignore the whole subject. The Anglican Church does not encourage morbid guilt feelings. But while avoiding the danger of becoming obsessed with our own sinfulness, we must also abandon any illusions of innocence. The church teaches that we are all sinners.

Sin should not be mistaken for a childish naughtiness which could easily be cured by a smack on the bottom. One of the simplest words for sin in the Bible is a word originally used to describe an archer's arrow falling short of the target. Since our target is to live in a loving relationship with God and each other, we can easily see how frequently we fall short of the target.

The sin which is most difficult to overcome is corporate sin. This kind of sin is beyond the control of any individual person. For example, it is obviously wrong and evil for some people to starve while others waste food or misuse resources which could produce food. It cannot be right for nations to spend vast sums on armaments yet make only pitifully small contributions toward providing clean water for the millions who suffer disease and poverty. Yet individuals and even whole nations can feel helpless and impotent when faced with economic, social, and political structures which support evil. We can all say, Don't blame me; I would change it if I could! But we must also admit that we enjoy temporary security because we are protected by the war machine's complicated balance of terror, and benefit in our standard of living because the third world is powerless to prevent exploitation.

You will be able to think of many other examples which will prove that human society is imperfect and falls very far short of the standard of divine love. This is corporate sin. You will also be able to list all kinds of ways in which corporate sin is destructive, because sin is always destructive. We dare not tolerate sin on the grounds that one cannot expect perfection and that unfortunately we always fall short of the target. The failure to love has drastic consequences, not because God is irritable and gets annoyed, but because in reality the ways of death and destruction are opposite to the ways of life and love.

When we focus our attention on individual and personal sins, we may think that all we need to correct our faults is a decision to mend our ways, and a little more willpower. Try again the exercise using 1 Corinthians 13. Even the best of us is a sinner when we measure ourselves beside Jesus. We might quite sensibly ask why we should set such a high standard for ourselves. The answer is twofold. First, individual sin is also destructive. When we think seriously about ourselves, we learn to recognize destructive tendencies in our personalities, thinking, and behaviour. When we are controlled by these tendencies instead of our tendencies toward love and perfection, we hurt ourselves and each other. Secondly, we are made for something better than sin, shoddiness, or even mere mediocrity. The sad truth is that many people are too humble to be penitent. They have such a low estimate of their potential that they suffer neither disappointment nor shame when they fall short of the mark. They have sold themselves short. If you see yourself as you really are and as God sees you, you will know that you have great potential for love and goodness. You will also recognize that you can do more damage and cause more hurt than you once so blindly or modestly assumed. If you believe your life is insignificant, you are not likely to feel the need to repent. When you become aware that God has made you for love and loves you personally, you will feel uncomfortable about sin.

When we can acknowledge that we are sinful persons in a sinful society, we are ready to look for salvation. Salvation means to be saved from danger or rescued from peril. When we think of sin as sickness, then salvation is healing. When we think of sin as bondage, then salvation is liberation or redemption. In the gospel the church tells us that even though we cannot save ourselves, God reaches out in love and saves us.

At the risk of oversimplifying we can say that on the basis of what we already know about God, it is only reasonable to expect that he would reach out to save us. He made us for love, and we must be free to love. When we fail in loving and misuse our freedom, we also lose our ability to use our freedom. The past failures of our society and ourselves enslave us and weigh us down. Since our love is too weak, God's love must reach us. It must reach us where we are and as we are. God entered human life in

Christ and bridged the gap. This kind of self-giving love is very costly. Love which is so deep feels all the pain of all the injuries which human failures have caused and allowed. In the crucifixion, when Jesus suffered and died on the cross, God in his love absorbed all the destructiveness of all our sin, and still his love triumphed over death.

You will learn more about salvation as you draw on the three fountains of Bible, prayer, and the sacraments. For now it is sufficient to emphasize that we are sinners, we need salvation, and God offers us salvation. Because his offer is an offer of love, we can either respond or ignore it. The vital thing is to be in a right relationship with God. We have described this as a loving relationship. When God saves us by re-establishing the bond of love, our salvation leads to our overcoming sin and moving toward our perfection, holiness, righteousness, and love.

Martin Luther once said that God shows his righteousness as a master-craftsman shows his craftsmanship. First of all, a master-craftsman points out his apprentices' faults. Secondly, he shows his apprentices a table, for example, which he has made and with which they can compare their imperfect attempts. But he has not really succeeded until he makes his apprentices like himself. Similarly, God in his righteousness shows us our sins. Then God in Jesus Christ shows us a perfect human life to which we can compare our lives. But the really good news is that God in his love, through his Spirit at work in us, makes us like himself if we let him.

When we become like God, our salvation is complete. The aim of creation, that we are the image of God and able to enter into a loving relationship with him, is restored. The aim of the incarnation, when God became man so that we might become like God, is achieved. The aim of the atonement, that God and man be at-one, is accomplished. The new life of the resurrection is lived in love that is eternal. The Holy Spirit of God, who is love, has been received, and we are sanctified (made holy).

History and Structure

Most of what I have written so far could have been said by a Roman Catholic or an Eastern Orthodox Christian. A great deal of it would be acceptable to a Protestant or a member of a Reformed Church. Anglicans would probably not like to think that they follow a peculiar or exotic brand of Christianity. But an observer of the Anglican phenomenon might detect some strong emphases, and a few eccentricities and idiosyncrasies, that blend with the basic Christian faith to give it an Anglican flavour. Of course you do not have to like or accept all a family's behaviour in order to belong to that family. A little history will help to explain a lot about our way and help you to understand and identify our community. If you read the history of the church, you will probably be well entertained, shocked, amused, instructed, inspired, and challenged. One of the emphases of Anglicanism is on history. Our way shows a great respect for the past.

Our story properly begins with creation, but it was Christ who founded the church, as we know it, to be the new Israel. He commissioned it to proclaim the gospel and entrusted its leadership to the apostles. In the beginning the church appeared to be a Jewish sect, but with the outstanding help of Saint Paul, it quickly spread among the Gentiles, who soon outnumbered Jewish Christians and became, as they remain, the overwhelming majority in the church. Until the early fourth century, when the Emperor Constantine became a Christian, Christianity was subject to periodic persecutions and received no encouragement from the secular authorities. The martyrs who died rather than deny their faith, left an indelible mark on subsequent church life. They were willing to die for love of Christ, confident that they would rise with him.

The conversion of the Emperor brought official recognition and the temptation to get involved in politics, ostensibly as the conscience of the state but too often to legitimize the status quo. However, the church continued to expand by taking the good news to those who had not heard it. To define doctrine and to decide on church practice, the bishops met in councils. The ecumenical councils of the undivided church are enormously important to all Catholic, Orthodox, and Anglican Christians.

The origins of Christianity in Britain are threefold. Christianity was established there but had little influence in the Roman period. Then Celtic missionaries preached the gospel to the north, and Augustine (of Canterbury) brought the good news to the south from Rome. Celtic customs gave way to the dominant Roman and Latin form of Western Christianity. The English church at this time and throughout the middle ages was an integral, highly respected, and dynamic part of Western Christendom.

While British Christianity remained part of the church in the West, quite a different expression of Christianity was experienced in the East. Instead of Latin, Greek thought and language were dominant. As the centuries passed, East and West drifted apart until Rome and Constantinople, representing the Western and Eastern branches of the one, holy, catholic, and apostolic church, broke off communion with each other in the eleventh century. That unhappy division still exists, although great efforts are now being made to reconcile the churches.

Medieval Europe, including Britain, saw a magnificent flowering of Christian culture. The typical Anglican church in Canada, however recently it was founded, will show the influence of the middle ages in architecture, stained glass, furniture, ornaments, vestments, embroidery, styles of worship, music, and theology.

In the sixteenth century the Protestant Reformation destroyed the unity of the Western church. Feeling the impact of the Renaissance, the influence of Protestant reformers in continental Europe, and a growing nationalism, the Church of England began a dispute over jurisdiction with the Bishop of Rome (the Pope) that has led to more than four centuries of divided and independent history.

The Church of England was not a new church established at the time of the Reformation, but the same ancient church that refused to accept the jurisdiction of the Bishop of Rome in England. It began a series of reforms that were intended to bring church life closer to the intentions of Christ and the practice of the early church. The most important benefits for the Anglican Church were a new translation of the Bible, with the encouragement of its widespread study, and the creation of a Prayer Book in English, which almost everybody could understand. The ancient form of church government and the ministry of bishops, priests, and deacons were preserved.

At this time a principle was established which has continued to be characteristically Anglican. This is the refusal to change merely for the sake of change but to have an enormous respect for tradition. If something to do with the church was clearly a corruption, an abuse, or destructive, then reform was appropriate. If something continued to be a vehicle of grace, then it was enthusiastically preserved. Customs which are relatively unimportant were allowed to survive if they could. This approach explains some of the curiosities of Anglicanism. For example, the clergy still dress for services as if trousers had not been invented. Their costume is dignified, sometimes colourful, rich with symbolism and historical associations, and emphasizes the ministry of Christ rather than the personality of the individual minister. Because there is no need to reform, it has remained more or less the same. Respect for the achievements, wisdom, customs, and even the eccentricities of the past is prominent in Anglicanism. Since we are not sure that we are wiser than our fathers, we are willing to learn from them. This reverent approach to tradition saved Anglicanism from discarding much of great value during periods of rapid and drastic change.

Having separated from Rome, the Church of England tried to be a catholic church with a strong emphasis on freedom of conscience, the importance of the Bible, and the traditional faith and order of the church. The Anglican Church also tried to welcome as many Christians as possible by avoiding divisive regulations which would exclude people unnecessarily. Anglicans were so successful at being comprehensive that many other Christians have difficulty in understanding how such a wide range of opinion and practice can be enjoyed in one communion. It is hard to explain, but it exists.

The Anglican Church took its part in the great era of missionary expansion and also extended its pastoral ministry to its members as they settled around the world. The result is the present multiracial, multicultural, and multilingual family of churches in the Anglican communion. The Anglican Church of Canada illustrates these two expansionary thrusts. Almost all of Canada's Eskimos and many of her Indians are Anglicans. So the voice and contribution of native people is very important to church life. The first recorded Anglican Communion service in Canada was at Frobisher Bay on 3 September 1578. Over the years since then the Anglican Church has achieved a reputation for offering the services of the church to isolated communities across this vast land.

While it is impossible to understand Anglicanism apart from our past, it is equally impossible to ignore our future. We believe that we have a future and that the future determines our direction and style in the present. There is a very creative tension between two valid views of the future. One is a historical future and the other is what we call an eschatological future. The historical view of the future is based on the confidence that the "gates of hell" will not prevail over the church, as Christ promised almost 2,000 years ago. The church believes it will worship God and serve his people for as long as human history continues. I used to be amused by the English Prayer Book's inclusion of a table to find the date of Easter until the year 2199 by a system of golden numbers and dominical letters. After living through some strange fads and crises, I now appreciate that long view of the future. People who figure out the date of Easter for two centuries hence are not likely to get flustered or go out of business because of temporary difficulties. Anglicans feel a loyalty to future generations as well as to those long past.

The other view of the future is quite different. Eschatology refers to the last things. We believe that we go to God, as we also come from him who is the Alpha and the Omega, the beginning and the end. This gives a mystical dimension to the present which, together with the past and future, is set in eternity and seen from that perspective. Eschatology is often expressed in visionary and poetic language. It sometimes appears to be talking about a dramatic end of the world which comes unexpectedly but not without warning. Beware of literal interpretations of lurid details and of any attempts to put eschatology on a time-line. In our view the future is not endless, meaningless, or cyclical. It has a direction which is determined by the loving purpose of God. There is a sense in which the uncertainty about when and how it will all end gives an exciting importance to every day. The confidence that "in the end there is God," takes away any fear about the last things. Lest you be discouraged or bewildered by eschatology, let me say that few people claim to understand this branch of theology.

One of the ancient traditions emphasized in the Anglican way is the observance of the Christian Year. A catholic way to experience the full gospel is to organize worship and teaching by a yearly calendar. At any given time you will find that some aspects of Christianity appeal to you more than others. Some important truths might be ignored altogether if they were not brought before us regularly. By a sequence of seasons, each with a special emphasis, the whole faith is presented in an annual cycle called the Christian Year.

The birth of Christ, his death and resurrection, and the coming of the Holy Spirit are celebrated at the high points of Christmas, Easter, and Pentecost. Leading up to and following these festivals is a marvellous pattern of teaching, with opportunities through sacraments and worship to experience the truth that is taught. The teaching of course is almost a byproduct. The purpose of the seasons is liturgical, to aid worship. When we fulfil our primary purpose, which is to glorify God, we most effectively achieve our secondary objective, which is to edify his people.

The best way to get the feel of the Christian Year is to go to church every Sunday for a year, plus Ash Wednesday, Good Friday, Ascension Day, and perhaps a few Saint's Days to remind us that we have some great examples to encourage us. This experience of a church year will bring to life the collects, epistles, and gospels which are provided in the Prayer Book for all Sundays and holy days. (Page 93 in the Prayer Book will give you an outline of how the Christian Year is arranged).

Anglicans are in favour of organized religion. Our way is to recognize the need for Christianity and the church to be organized. We focus our organization in the bishops. This is why some branches of the Anglican communion use the word *episcopal* rather than *Anglican* in their official name.

In the first generation of the church there was no immediate need for written gospels or much formal organization. But if the mission and message of God in Christ were to be faithfully shared with succeeding generations, then there had to be reliable and recognized scriptures and institutions to preach the gospel, administer the sacraments, and care for the church. The bishops were the successors of the apostles, and they still maintain and exercise the apostolic ministry. They are responsible for the doctrine, sacraments, and discipline of Christ.

Bishops can only be consecrated (ordained) by other bishops, although they may be chosen by an election at a diocesan synod, as in Canada, or nominated in other ways. To safeguard continuity and ensure suitability, at least three bishops must assist in consecrating a new bishop. Properly consecrated bishops are said to be in the apostolic succession and the historic episcopate.

Bishops serve a geographical area known as a diocese, and share the ministry of that diocese with priests and deacons whom they ordain. Every baptized Christian in the diocese also has a ministry and shares the worship, witness, and service of the church. We have a system of synods in which lay members, clergy, and bishops pray, consult, and plan for the good of the church, and make what few laws are necessary for our well being.

Some people find it strange that we have an apparently democratic system of government by synods, existing alongside an apparently undemocratic system of rule by bishops. It is a complex question, but two clues will help. First, the aim of both the synodical and the episcopal systems is to respond to God's call and guidance, to obey him, and to serve his people. Our aim is theocratic. If we are getting it right, there can be no conflict. Secondly, because the aim of the whole organization is love, and love cannot live without freedom, freedom is guarded and encouraged by both systems which in practice support and enrich each other. Like a lot of things about Anglicanism, our government may look strange on paper but it works fairly well in practice.

The basic unit of the Anglican Church is the diocese. Dioceses are linked with each other and the rest of the worldwide church through provinces. In Canada four ecclesiastical provinces comprising thirty dioceses compose one national church with a general synod led by an archbishop called the Primate. The general synod and provincial synods have legislative powers.

Partly because of our continuing disagreement with Rome over the nature and extent of papal authority, and partly because we believe it is better to encourage the maximum freedom to respond to the Spirit's guidance, there is no central jurisdictional authority for the whole

Anglican communion. We manage to enjoy unity and encourage cooperation by fraternal exchanges and consultations such as the Lambeth Conference of Bishops and the Anglican Consultative Council.

Returning to the diocese you will find that it is subdivided into parishes. A parish is only a sub-unit and is incomplete apart from the diocese. For example, all seven sacraments could not be administered without the bishop. A congregation, worshipping, witnessing, and serving, is the cutting edge of the church. It is the front line where the action is, but it is always nourished by, and must always support, the wider church. So freedom to be the church in the most effective way in a particular local situation is encouraged. But what we call congregationalism or parochialism that ignores or weakens the wider family, is resisted.

A parish is normally served by a parish priest appointed by the bishop. In Canada the priest is usually called the rector, and the parish generally has some say in the choice of a new rector. Typically the rector will appoint one of the parishioners to be a churchwarden, and the parishioners will elect another churchwarden. The two churchwardens and the rector have great power and freedom in the exercise of their responsibility for the leadership and maintenance of parish life. Usually they will be supported and advised by a parish council elected by the annual meeting of all parishioners. At the annual meeting, which is usually called the vestry meeting, elections are held, a budget is adopted, and major policies and programs are discussed. Like the diocese the parish tries to combine democratic and hierarchical approaches to making decisions.

Supported by parishes and dioceses there are many special ministries and programs of the Anglican Church. Hospitals, universities, schools, missionary work, social service and action, world relief and development are only a few of the areas where the church has both paid and volunteer workers. Very important also are the religious orders of monks and nuns, and the Church Army which does evangelistic, social service, and pastoral work. Many tasks are best undertaken in cooperation with other denominations, and there are many interchurch coalitions, a list of whose names would look like alphabet soup. You can become effectively involved in almost any area of service to God's people and his world through your membership in the body of Christ.

Another aspect of our Anglican way is our use of many ancient terms. This is not surprising when you remember how old we are. Sometimes it is difficult to find new and different words to express old and lasting truths. Do not be discouraged if you find that after six months or a year you still come across quaint or archaic terms which mean nothing to you. If your curiosity gets the better of you, then find out the meaning of offending words. Good sources of information are an English dictionary, your parish priest (who probably loves explaining our language), and *A Concise Dictionary of Ecclesiastical Terms* by F.L. Eckel.

Authority

The teachings and practice of the Anglican Church are thoroughly reliable. They are trustworthy because they are securely based on scriptures, tradition, and reason. Like our three fountains of living water, all three sources of authority are essential. Scripture, tradition, and reason are not mutually exclusive, but each relies upon the other two for strength and light. The probability of error in our understanding increases enormously if we rely on only one source. For instance, if you ignore tradition and refuse to use your reason when you read the Bible, you may find superstition instead of true religion.

The scriptures are enormously important because they record the historical encounter of God with men. Although the scriptures are authoritative in the Anglican Church, we base our teaching and practice not on isolated passages but on the Bible as a whole. There would not be a Bible unless the church had assembled it. The church decided which writings were authoritative and included them in what we call the canon of scripture. The church then preserved and passed on the scriptures. The value of the scriptures, however, is not what the church gave to them but what the church saw in them. So the church, in receiving the scriptures, acknowledges them as the gift of God. The Anglican Church will not teach anything to be necessary for salvation unless it can plainly be proved from the Bible.

The word *tradition* has two distinct meanings: that which was "handed over" and that which is "handed down.'' The first meaning, handed over, refers to the revelation of God to and through the prophets and apostles. In this sense tradition is fixed and is found in the scriptures, which contain God's revealed word and the basis of the sacraments and creeds. It is the mission of the church to preserve this original deposit of tradition and to hand it over to the living church community, in a way that can be accepted, experienced, and understood.

The second meaning of tradition, handed down, refers to the accumulated wisdom of nearly twenty Christian centuries. The insights and experiences of our predecessors, in their successes and failures, form a vast treasury on which we can draw. Often their insights provide us with interpretations of the handed over tradition. The church with its long experience enables us to receive the original deposit and to understand it. The living tradition also hands down other insights. We must be consistent with God's revelation in the scriptures and in Christ, but we must also be prepared to learn from the Holy Spirit's guiding us over the centuries and today. A lot of our traditions are things we have learned since the first century. This tradition is so wide ranging that some parts are emphasized and some almost forgotten in each age. We sometimes appear to be a large house with a big attic in which all kinds of fascinating things are stored just in case they might be useful one day.

Some traditions are more important than others. The doctrine of the Trinity is an example of an essential tradition. The doctrine was not defined until the Council of Nicea in A.D. 325. It was expressed more precisely at the

Council of Constantinople in A.D. 381. The way in which we have received it was influenced by Saint Augustine at the beginning of the fifth century and perhaps most clearly described by Saint Thomas Aquinas in the thirteenth century. Today theologians are struggling to find a contemporary way of talking about God. However daring and innovative a scholar is, the church will insist that the new insights and expressions of scholarship must acknowledge God's revelation of himself as the one, holy, and undivided Trinity before the new can become part of the church's teaching. This is a case where the original revelation is protected and proclaimed by the living tradition.

We can exercise far more freedom with traditions like the sacrament of confirmation, which has been handled very differently over the centuries and between East and West. How it is done is a matter of church discipline guided by tradition seeking to discover the most effective way of receiving divine grace in the contemporary situation.

More liberties can be taken with other traditions. In the case of our musical traditions great variety is permitted. Not that music is unimportant. As poetry takes us beyond prose, so music takes us beyond words in worship. Music enriches and illuminates our liturgies. Generally the Anglican view is that, because worship is offered to God, all music should be the best we can offer. Because worship is the offering of the people, the musical style will vary with the worshipping congregation. Anglicans have a tradition of church music of which they are enormously proud. By the time we get to this kind of tradition, questions of authority are less important.

In summary, to be confident in our interpretation of what was handed over, we rely on the understandings that have been handed down in the living church. We live richer lives because the tradition grows. If we are responsive to the Spirit in today's world, we shall contribute to the tradition received by tomorrow's church. While we are grateful for new insights, they are always judged by the normative revelation of God in Christ.

The source of authority that is reason is important to humanity as a whole. Some people try to oppose reason to religion. There are even some Christian groups who seem to encourage this misguided conflict by adopting a strongly anti-intellectual stance. When Jesus was a boy, he learned from the law of Moses in the scriptures to love God with all his faculties, including his mind. In his teachings as a man, he repeated the command to love God with all our mind. We thank God for the gift of reason, and we are commanded to use it. Notice that reason is seen in the commandment as an expression of love for God.

We are expected to use our common sense and our critical faculties when we study scripture and receive tradition. We are also expected to be reasonable enough to examine the evidence of scripture and tradition. A rationalist who dismisses as worthless the experience of countless millions of his contemporaries and predecessors, is not being reasonable but arrogant. So we are expected to be honest, open to the truth, and willing to work hard mentally. Not every Christian is expected to engage in technical theological research. But just as the church respects and encourages the use of the individual conscience, so the church reverences and asks us to use our intellects. Because we are not isolated individuals but persons in community, we exercise reason in dialogue with other rational beings. Because we believe that God is the source of all truth and seeks to reveal himself to us, the church has nothing to fear and a great deal to gain from the use of reason.

When we know that our way is based on the Bible, on tradition, and on reason, we can walk confidently. When we actually experience the church as the agent of the living God, we can walk with cosmic confidence. The Anglican way is marked by respect for the past, confidence in the present, and openness to the future. Rooted in scripture, tradition, and reason, its ultimate authority is the divine authority shared by all other Christian communions.

Basic Steps

This book is meant for "immigrants," not "tourists." I hope you will live in the church community and not just look at it. If you are serious about citizenship, may I suggest a few basic steps.

1   Acquire a Bible, a Prayer Book, and a parish church immediately, and use all three regularly.

2   As soon as you are ready to make a commitment, tell Jesus you want to follow him and you want him to be Lord of your life.

3   If you are not already baptized and confirmed, approach your parish priest and ask to be prepared for these sacraments. You will then be able to draw freely on all three fountains of living water, the Bible, prayer, and the sacraments.

4   Discipleship is costly. Be prepared to make changes and sacrifices.

5   Become active in some service to the church and to your fellow men.

6   Take your Christianity seriously. Work hard at it. But don't be too serious. God has a sense of humour. Over thirty years ago my parish priest told me that if my religion made me miserable I should give it up. I think he was safe giving that advice, because the Anglican way will not make us miserable.

7   Ask a parish priest or other experienced Christian to be your spiritual adviser.

8   Don't expect to be wildly enthusiastic all the time. On a journey from here to eternity you are bound to pass

through humdrum, tranquil, tumultuous, and exciting times. May God bless you on your way.

Suggested Books

Eckel, Frederick L. Jr. *A Concise Dictionary of Ecclesiastical Terms* (New York: Abingdon Press, 1960).

Neil, William. *One Volume Bible Commentary* (Toronto: Hodder and Stoughton, 1978).

Neill, Stephen. *Anglicanism* (London: Mowbrays, 1977).